D1441195

WINTER'S JOURNEY

POETRY BY STEPHEN DOBYNS

Winter's Journey

Mystery, So Long

The Porcupine's Kisses

Pallbearers Envying the One Who Rides

Common Carnage

Velocities: New and Selected Poems, 1966–1992

Body Traffic

Cemetery Nights

Black Dog, Red Dog

The Balthus Poems

Heat Death

Griffon

Concurring Beasts

Winter's Journey

STEPHEN DOBYNS

COPPER CANYON PRESS

Port Townsend, Washington

Many thanks are due the editors of the following publications, in which this work first appeared.

The American Poetry Review: "Balance," "Ducks," and "Possum."
Journal of New Jersey Poets: "Napatree Point."
The Kenyon Review: "Mourning Doves" and "Nickel."
Narrative: "Lost," "Poem," and "Rabbits."
Ploughshares: "Chainsaws."
Poetry International: "Spring."

Most of these poems were begun in the winter of 2007 and were affected by that season's political climate. I would like to thank friends whose suggestions helped make these poems better: Hayden Carruth, Joe-Anne McLaughlin Carruth, Louise Glück, Thomas Lux, Ellen Bryant Voigt, and C.K. Williams.

Copyright 2010 by Stephen Dobyns
All rights reserved
Printed in the United States of America

Cover art: Photograph by Stephen Dobyns

Copper Canyon Press is in residence at Fort Worden State Park in Port Townsend, Washington, under the auspices of Centrum. Centrum is a gathering place for artists and creative thinkers from around the world, students of all ages and backgrounds, and audiences seeking extraordinary cultural enrichment.

LIBRARY OF CONGRESS CATALOGING-IN-PUBLICATION DATA

Dobyns, Stephen, 1941–
Winter's journey / Stephen Dobyns.
  p. cm.
ISBN 978-1-55659-305-5 (pbk.: alk. paper)
I. Title.
PS3554.O2W56 2010
811'.54—dc22

                                                      2010004641

9 8 7 6 5 4 3 2 FIRST PRINTING

COPPER CANYON PRESS
Post Office Box 271
Port Townsend, Washington 98368
www.coppercanyonpress.org

for Isabel

CENTRAL ARKANSAS LIBRARY SYSTEM
LITTLE ROCK PUBLIC LIBRARY
100 ROCK STREET
LITTLE ROCK, ARKANSAS 72201

CONTENTS

WINTER'S JOURNEY

POEM

Who has the time? he asked.
But none in the room wore a watch.

On the hearth lay a dog, its two
front paws making parallel lines.

It's eleven o'clock, said another,
the day has scarcely begun.

But the dog was a black dog,
black with one blind eye.

It's nearing midnight, said a third,
and which of us is ready?

NAPATREE POINT

A mile from where I live is a beach where in winter
I walk the dog, console myself with the ocean's beauty,
and ponder the imponderables, like what to do about
living in a country that has become an embarrassment,
disliked and even hated around the world, a constant
source of bickering among its people and led by men
and women who seem stupid, but are probably only
scared, greedy, egotistical, and ignorant. Forgive me
if I forget a few. How it got that way and what to do
becomes one of the imponderables and can keep me
busy for a long walk, while being unable to work out
an explanation makes me feel like a Good German
of the late 1930s. I mean, if only I thought the FBI
were tapping my phone, I'd take it as a compliment.
Regrettably the commissars of modern poetry don't
like poems to talk about bloodshed and babies blown
to smithereens, so I expect I should hold my tongue.
Not so long ago Harvard's top poetry critic told me
and a few others that she took pride in never once
having voted. It was hard to feel more than sad, but,
to me, she vanished, she became a nonperson, as if
she had walked out on the human race, her writings

also, since what truth could she say about poetry if
she separated poetry from the world? I know I can't
just rant in a poem, although it's hard to stop myself,
but given the problem I hate going back to writing
about flowers and sex. Yet none of that affects being
ashamed of the country in which one lives and not
knowing how to fix it. The Great Twitterer is famous
for saying poetry makes nothing happen, other things
also, but even if that were the case, one must, I think,
still raise one's voice. It would be dreadful to be merely
a Good German, turning my back as Jews were carted off.
Is it the enormity of the daily calamity that makes so many
contemporary poets write lines without meaning or use
language to hide meaning? Take Ashbery, for instance,
not to beat a dead horse, and surely other names might
do as well, but is nonmeaning intended to obscure
the awfulness of meaning, just as Dadaists made snappy
responses to World War I? At times it seems the only
sane answer is a joke. Even slapstick can be an answer,
as if to slip on a banana might form a rational response
to the trenches of the Somme. But despite the jokes,
nonmeaning seems a kind of shirking, to duck what
somebody lacks the capacity to express. And the value
of nonmeaning? Totally zip. Do you see how these
imponderables can get a grip? In a letter, Chekhov wrote
that he didn't need to say stealing horses was wrong,
he only had to describe a horse thief exactly. But even

Chekhov couldn't write about the czar without landing
in a Russian clink. That at least tells us a lot about
the power of language in Russia, whereas I could write
about the president to my heart's content and not make
the slightest dent on the escutcheon of his indifference,
which is still no reason to write about flowers and sex.
So in fact it's the frustration of being unable to describe
the horror without just shouting, Look at the horror!
I mean, people aren't dumb. Even if they turn away
to scribble non sequiturs they know something nasty
is creeping up behind them. How these imponderables
can age us, like dragging a dead horse up a mountain:
what do I get but a dead horse up a mountain? And I'm
still no closer to understanding how to live in a country
that's become an embarrassment, which occurs in part
from weighing the idealism of the Constitution against
the cynicism of the present administration, much like
comparing a bathing beauty to a drag queen, which is
not to insult drag queens. But what to do except make
inept and fretful remarks remains unclear when really
I'd like to skirt the defects of language and hurl a rock—
another useless gesture meant to make me feel better.
Were I walking along that winter beach I would now
have walked a mile at least with nothing to show for it
but a wrinkled brow and a vague wringing of hands,
while the question remains as fresh as ever—what
to do about the horror? Then the subject is no longer
about a solution but about the question itself hanging

in the air at the end of Napatree Point with the surf beating against it, not to wear it down, but to keep it bright, till at last I whistle for the dog and walk back.

DUCKS

for David Fenza

Warm in my truck by the lighthouse at Watch Hill
on a sunny morning in midwinter, I observe
the ducks bobbing among ice-covered rocks
and think of Bashō and what his position might
have been on the subject of the demand-side
economics of poetry, a term I have just learned,
which argues that the smaller a poet's number
of readers, the less reason the poet has to write,
and why bother if not a single line will stick
in the mind a nanosecond past the poet's death?
And I also wonder about these ducks and why
their feet don't get frozen down there among
the chunks of ice, or maybe they only seem not
to get frozen and instead the ducks are very brave
as they seek out sweet things to eat, or sweet
for a duck. Bashō wrote: I feel when I sit with
Kikaku at a party that he is anxious to compose
a verse that will delight the entire company,
while I have no such wish. Bashō of course said
this in Japanese, which I know as much about
as I know about the feet of ducks. As for Kikaku,
he is recalled only for once being mentioned
by Bashō, despite his faith in the demand-side

economics of poetry. On ducks, Bashō wrote:
Sea darkening—the wild duck's cry is dimly white.
This morning the ducks have been joined by terns,
cormorants, and gulls. There's good eating if you
don't mind diving for it and don't mind the cold.
The day is so clear I can almost count the trees
on Block Island eight miles away. I doubt Bashō
when writing a poem ever said: This will knock
their socks off. But he *did* write: Eat vegetable
soup rather than duck stew. Which wasn't meant
to keep ducks from being eaten, but expressed
his belief in simplicity—plainness and oddness
being qualities he liked. Across the narrow strip
of land to the lighthouse the wind blows so hard
that a seagull by my truck has to beat its wings
like crazy just to stay in one spot. Many times
my life feels like that, lots of work just to stay put.
Bashō said that within him was something like
a windswept spirit that when he was young took
to writing poetry merely to amuse itself at first,
but then at last becoming its lifelong occupation.
At times it grew so dejected that it nearly quit,
at other times it grew so swollen with pride that
it rejoiced in vain victories over others. Barthes
in an essay claimed that writers are driven only
by vanity, which is why they must appear in print,
and maybe this fuels the demand-side economics
of poetry, the wish for a kiss-me-kiss-me response.

Like most lighthouses, this one is a white pillar
of stone with a beacon on top, but surely it's no
longer needed, since ships don't come this close
and all have radar—even small boats would be
warned away by the buoys. In the fog, its horn
makes a moan like a cow mourning for her calf
and its light slowly rotates like an exploratory eye,
but the whole business could be knocked down
and sold to developers, which makes good sense
if you buy into the demand-side theory of life.
Bashō said that ever since his windswept spirit
began to write poetry it never felt at peace with itself
but was prey to all sorts of doubts. Once it wanted
the security of a job at court and once it wanted
to measure the depths of its ignorance by becoming
a scholar. I know I haven't read as much as I might,
but it seems the demand-side folks and Barthes
are leaving out a big part of the argument. A poet
has a complicated emotion and produces a poem;
a duck has a complicated emotion and produces
an egg. The demand-side case says they differ just
in the nature of their product, poem versus egg,
and both could fetch the same price at the market.
Off to my left float two brightly colored mallards;
to my right are three brown ducks, clearly females.
They appear to be ignoring one another, but perhaps
I'm wrong, perhaps they shoot quick sexual glances
in each other's direction and soon they will head

back to the marsh and create an egg. And good
for them, I say, the world could use more ducks.
What other creature so aptly describes a doctor?
Bashō also wrote: Cold night—the wild duck, sick,
falls from the sky and sleeps awhile. And he said
he didn't become a courtier or scholar because
his unquenchable love of poetry held him back.
In fact, this windswept spirit knew no other art
than the art of writing poetry, and consequently,
it clung to it, he said, more or less blindly. At times
I repeat those last words to myself: *more or less
blindly.* Maybe many people would consider this
a bleak picture of the poet's work, but in me
it awakens a sense of excitement, as when you love
to eat turkey bladders and then one day you meet
somebody else who loves to eat turkey bladders
and you feel you could talk to this person forever
and never grow bored. And I'm glad that Bashō
didn't say the product or purpose was the poem's
future life, but instead the product was the writing,
that Bashō was writing the poem for itself alone—
as reckless as that seems—and not for any future
profit. Doesn't this put Bashō into the category
of nutcase, just as a person with an intense passion
for turkey bladders might be called a nutcase?
Sitting in my truck, looking out past the ducks,
out past Block Island and into the Atlantic, perhaps
in the direction of France, I see the water is a much

darker blue than in summer, as if the cold added
an extra layer of color. The white tips of the waves
look more like ice or snow than flecks of froth.
How long could I watch without growing bored?
Maybe until I got hungry or needed to pee. As for
why ducks don't get cold feet, to me it's a mystery,
though I'll wager books are written on the subject,
just as books get written on the motivation of poets
and why they bother. A little ways from shore, light
reflects off the water as if from the sun's hand mirror,
and I like to believe that shortly there will emerge
from the iridescence, more or less blindly, a small
boat carrying an aged Japanese poet, at which point
I'll jump from my truck into the wind's whirling
ambiguity and shout and wave my hat over my head.
Nothing is rational about this and it's something
about which I should maybe keep my mouth shut,
but it's an event the ducks and I hope to see happen,
not for profit, mind you, just for the thing itself.

RHINOCEROS

Snow in the early morning, then sleet by dawn,
switching to steady rain by eight. I like to see
the weather flexing its muscles. Now the wind
is picking up from the north, lashing the rain
into a radical slant. There's not a bird in sight.
Today is Valentine's Day, named for a saint
who most likely didn't exist. Like love itself,
perhaps, here today, gone tomorrow. Earlier
this morning I drove to the florist as cars slid
across the ice as elegantly as Olympic skaters.
Soon I came back with two cyclamens, their heart-
shaped leaves marking them as a Valentine gift:
purple for my daughter, bright red for my wife.
Nothing else today has such color, although
I see a wide variety of gray. My wife arrived
in this country on Valentine's Day twenty-three
years ago. Ten months later our daughter was born.
I wish I could say that it has always been easy,
but the good times have offset the bad by maybe
ten to one. And that's pretty good, right? I mean,
that's maybe as good as it gets. And if someone
does a little better, I don't want to hear about it.
At least I've never felt regret, while each time

she crosses my line of sight feels like a gift, and,
sure, there are other pleasures, though I'd prefer
not to reveal too much. What are those animals
that live all by themselves and come out only
to have sex? Rhinos, for example. Collectively
they're called a *crash* of rhinos, which doesn't
sound reassuring. So would it surprise anybody
that rhinos aren't famous for having friends?
But at times I think I should have lived like that,
hunkered down in my rhino den and feeling sullen
as I sharpened my horn on a rock, but, believe me,
it wouldn't have meant happiness or even pleasure,
just teeth-clenched endurance. And if I did it,
what would be the point? But I'm lying to myself.
I have no wish to be a rhino. Where does such self-
deception come from? Yet when I see my wife
sitting across the room and it feels like a gift,
part of me thinks I should hurry to my rhino den
and chomp on some moldy grass. Megafauna
is how they're classified, and odd-toed ungulates.
Can you imagine as a kid telling Aunt Betty
when she asked about your future, I want to grow up
to be a megafauna? But the real reason I never
told Aunt Betty was cowardice. I lacked the courage
to face her stricken disappointment or lively scorn.
Early rhinos weighed twelve tons, twice the weight
of elephants, and we should be glad they all became
extinct. Even these days in India and Nepal rhinos

kill more people than tigers and leopards combined.
Not only do rhinos feel sullen, they feel obviously
aggrieved. What the baby rhino hoped for and what
it got left it in a permanent bad mood. A two-hour-old
baby rhino I saw once looked like a leather hassock.
It's a big leap from hassock to oversized megafauna.
Why I would tell Aunt Betty I wanted to be a rhino
isn't clear to me. I mean, it seems like something
at the edge of psychosis. But this morning driving
to the florist and watching the cars skid around,
I saw that being a rhino was like being an SUV
and what I'd been seeking was a sense of safety,
which, when looked at logically, might make sense
but my choice of animal was silly, and it wasn't just
safety that I wanted but a sense of self-sufficiency,
like being your own Swiss Army knife, but bigger.
But could I tell my wife I had doubts about shared
domesticity on account of my wish to be an SUV,
like telling her I wanted a sex-change, but worse?
And it's not even true, I don't want to be an SUV,
but, no matter how much I love her, a nervous voice
still nags in my ear: You'd be better off as an SUV
or best of all a rhino, one of those twelve-ton ones
nobody would mess with. The root of this desire
is a total mystery to me. I don't really like rhinos.
I don't have a collection of rhino figurines or keep
their pictures on my dresser or display them proudly
on T-shirts as people do with dogs, pigs, and bears.

Nevertheless the nervous voice tries to convince me
this is wisdom; I mean, not even the nervous voice
likes rhinos, it's just, to his mind, a best-case scenario.
And even if tempted by SUVs, he prefers rhinos more,
since they can live about fifty years and don't make
much noise other than stamping their three-toed feet.
All sorts of people treat their foibles with affection,
as they might treat a dim-witted child with affection.
Oh, I always mix ice cream, catsup, and beer, they say,
with a laugh that invites you to laugh along as well.
But you can't do that if you want to be a rhino. Sorry,
I must stop saying that; I've really no wish to be a rhino.
You know how it can happen when your brain knows
one thing and another part of your body thinks it knows
something else, perhaps it's in the stomach or spleen,
or in one of those glands? Like my urge to be a rhino
is caused by my endocrine glands or exocrine glands,
while my brain tries to keep me on a safer and more
sensible course. But if I were to tell this to my wife
as the reason why I sometimes seem distant or why
I have a fear of being happy, she'd give me the look
people make before they spit. And she's a scientist,
she speaks mathematics like Finns speak Finnish.
So it would be tough to convince her. Yet what I call
feeling distant or a worry of being happy turns into
the belief that I should hunker down in a rhino den.
I mean, the safer I feel, the more vulnerable I feel,
which is exactly how I feel when I use a chainsaw.

Some things you should never tell another person,
like turning to a stranger in a bar and confessing
you like to eat cow pies, it's just a bad idea. Even
if you confessed it to a priest in the confessional,
you'd regret it. Even if he didn't tell anyone else,
one day you'd catch him looking at you strangely.
A desire to be a rhino in a rhino den is like that,
but I swear I've no such wish, it's just a hankering
caused by a rogue gland, a hankering that makes
every other part of my body shout out, No! No!
But who would believe me? A fear of being happy,
a wish for an unattainable self-sufficiency, a fear
of vulnerability, which leads to isolation and being
short on trust. You see, I've already said too much.
By now it's nearly dark. The sun sets by five fifteen,
but on a gray day like this it hurries to get a head start
and by four o'clock it's grown so dark I can't tell
whether it's raining or what the wind is doing. Neither
the dog nor cat want to go out. And it's Valentine's
Day and I've given my wife flowers and chocolates
and told her I loved her and now I'm telling her
that part of me, a very small part, almost a smidgen,
wants to be a rhino hunkered down in a rhino den,
but why that should be the case, I just don't know.

MOURNING DOVES

The mourning doves are back earlier this year
with their call of patient lamentation, flying up
from the Carolinas after scarcely three months
away. My mother always disliked them, although
she knew the names of only a few birds: sparrows,
robins, cardinals, crows. Yet the mourning dove
she heard before the rest and it brought to mind
those friends and family members she had loved
and who had died and, clearly, as she got older,
that number got bigger so the dove's call became
a greater burden, especially after my father's death.
She would bend her head to hear the sound and then
shake her head to push it away. As for the bird itself,
only the male has a call and as one might suspect
it has to do with sex; and since the birds produce
up to six broods a season that's a lot of lamentation.
Now when I hear a dove, it's as if I hear my mother's
grief, which then calls back my own, although it's been
ten years since her death. My mother taught history
and liked its odd details, as when Peter the Hermit
led a crusade to Jerusalem and for good luck hundreds
of his followers each plucked a hair from his burro
until the beast was nearly bald. Others drank Peter's

bathwater just to make sure the good luck stuck,
which it didn't since most were soon slaughtered
by the Turks. Back then fake prophets were as thick
as leaves on an oak, as they had visions, preached
salvation, and urged their followers to kill the Jews
to ensure redemption. In time they would be hanged
or burned at the stake; then a new prophet would
arrive in town and new visions would get people
marching again, eager victims of bogus information
and ruthless ignorance. I would hope that ignorance
had lessened in a thousand years, but many Americans
still think evolution is an atheist plot and the earth
is six thousand years old—Jonestown, the Rapture
Index, a senator calling global warming "the greatest
hoax ever perpetrated on the American people."
What I like about birds is they lead simpler lives,
digging up worms and showing off their songs.
Perhaps one robin is more ignorant than the next,
but how could you tell? I have a CD of birdcalls,
and when I played it, the cat hurried into the room
with a hopeful expression, but then he caught on
and gave me a look that said, You got me again,
asshole. Like the time I made him elevate four feet
off the floor by giving my crow call a sharp toot right
behind his back. Mourning doves divvy up the work:
the male sits on the eggs in the morning and afternoon,
the female takes evening and night. At first they feed
their squabs pigeon milk or crop milk—old cells shed

from the crop wall and whooped up for the little ones.
It looks like yellow cottage cheese but is said to be tasty.
But listen, mourning doves always know what to do
and they repeat it year after year, while we tend to be
erratic. The trouble with having a mind that includes
an imagination, a sense of possibility, and a flexible
grasp of cause and effect is it can lead to astonishing
pinnacles of human achievement and incredible lows,
like the woman who found the Virgin Mary in a grilled
cheese sandwich, saying: "I went to take a bite and saw
this lady looking back." Ten years later she sold it
for twenty-eight thousand bucks to an online casino
that wants to take the sandwich on a world tour. This
is not uncommon. A couple in Nebraska have a pretzel
showing the Virgin holding the baby Jesus; a fellow
in Nashville displayed a cinnamon bun with the face
of Mother Teresa and a woman in L.A. found the face
of Jesus on the furry ass of a terrier mix named Angus.
Birds don't act like this. Lacking a sense of the possible
they are protected from an overreaching imagination.
Today in the yard birds were making springtime noises,
although it's only the end of February. Mourning doves
make sloppy nests and often put their sticks in some
inappropriate spot. They even build nests on the ground
or sneak their eggs into the better nests of other birds,
but, having done this almost forever, it's hard to call it
ignorance. It can't be compared to praying to the tuft
of fur on a terrier's ass. A friend claims that government,

mostly the right wing, has worked for years to dumb
down the population by cutting the quality of education
and reducing people's ability to tell the difference
between certainty, probability, possibility, and bullshit.
They do this by cutting funds for classes that teach
history and the arts, which decrease a sense of cause
and effect, so people grow more disposed to speeches
fobbing off the feasible or mistaken for the probable
or certain. And why the arts? Because they expand
a sense of what's possible. In fact, I think my friend
is right. It's easy for a government to convince voters
that to invest money in better schools is a bad idea,
just as salesmen can sell a gizmo to wash my floors,
groom a dog, and brush my teeth all at the same time.
Maybe I'm straying from what's said to be said in a poem,
but where does such an opinion come from? Probably
from poor schools and the limitations that mediocrity
puts on possibility, making up rules that seem right
because they've been repeated till one wants to puke.
But don't think I don't like the cat. Inside, he's a pal,
but outside he hunts the birds, so at times I shy a stone
in his direction and duck so he'll blame it on the hand
of God. Although my mother disliked mourning doves,
she disliked cats even worse, because they liked to eat
the mourning doves. If she found a cat in the yard
she would hurry out and shout, Shoo! But yesterday
my cat caught a mourning dove, maybe an ignorant one,
and again I thought of my mother. At times I wonder

what she would have said of our current administration
and praying to a cinnamon bun. Not that I imagine
her indignation, but I miss our conversations. She had
energetic political beliefs of the kind the right wing
calls liberal and liked to send off letters to the paper
about some politician's misreading of the Constitution.
I don't know, maybe she's lucky not knowing about
the holy grilled cheese sandwich and cinnamon bun.
Sorry, sorry, I'm getting off the subject again, being
guilty of writing about politics and furry terrier butts
when, really, that's not my intention. This is an elegy.

RABBITS

The sun boosts itself up from beyond the ocean,
initially just a glow, then a sliver of red. As it rises,
the light descends across the town, first touching
the narrow, nineteenth-century church steeples,
so briefly the steeples turn golden, while the rest
of the town stays dim. If I were religious I'd take
the illuminated steeples as a symbol of God's
engagement with the world, but being nonreligious
they stay a secular pleasure. As the light moves down,
the tips of winter trees begin to shine, then the light
touches the rooftops and the day gets underway.
But if I'm depressed, I don't see the light. It's just
a distraction, even an irritation. But today I saw it
and I slowed my truck to get a better look. It's back-
breaking work to keep alive one's feeling of delight
when one has no doubt about the world's constant
acts of ugliness, the greed of small-minded men,
and the brutality of time's unbroken progression.
Among my gifts the one I try to encourage most
is a sense of wonder, surely a minor talent and one
that gets a little creaky, but it's a gift that lets me
greet the day with a blend of pleasure and surprise.
Regrettably, I lack the emotional dexterity to greet

each day in this way, but I greet a decent number,
even if the talent comes with the bother of falling
victim to the sentimental so my eyes mist over
at the sugary adagio of a string quartet. Long ago
as a reporter I envied the cynicism of the men
with whom I worked. They had a clarity of vision,
or so I thought, that let them see through another's
hyperbole and deceit, to grasp what they supposed
to be the truth. Often they were right, but the only one
who kept his sense of wonder intact was a man who
wrote about the Detroit Zoo and got drunk each night
just to protect his eccentric delight. His favorite animal
was a gorilla that happened to be a world-class pitcher
of gorilla turds, and I could see this reporter wished he
could do that too, haul off and pitch a turd at anyone
who caused him aggravation, an editor for instance.
But for many reporters their cynicism became a canker
and their question about anybody, saint or sinner, was
what's in it for him, what's this guy trying to hide?
The chance of virtue or decency was rarely an option;
indeed, it was an anxiety. For years I've tried to balance
cynicism and wonder, like balancing a brick and a feather,
and I'm sorry to say that often I've fallen on the side
of the former. Each day during this February cold spell
the river has gradually frozen over and this morning
in the snow just beyond the riverbank I saw tracks
where two rabbits had taken a shortcut to Connecticut

across the ice. Even though I wished them luck, I felt
their chances slight. Kant wrote that what separates
human beings from other creatures is their ability
to distinguish between the actual and the possible.
So the right brain imagines a future event and the left
works out the logic, the left being a nuts-and-bolts
kind of creature, while the right is poised between
metaphor and dream, letting it speculate on what
doesn't exist. The rabbits crossing the river never
calculated the risk and just hopped ahead, while if I
stood at that spot, I'd say, I better not, being able
to picture the ice breaking and various nasty results.
But the left brain can obstruct information coming
from the right. So the cynic who bases his argument
on faulty logic can block a contrary notion, block
a sense of wonder, simply to protect his scaffolding
of bogus belief. At the paper I knew a reporter who
boasted about a death row convict he'd stared down
as the man was being strapped into an electric chair,
when he was an AP reporter in the South. He fixed
his gaze and the imminent corpse lowered his head,
abashed. This same reporter, in the bar late at night,
would recite "Casey at the Bat" and parts of *Cyrano
de Bergerac* — his tough-guy trappings temporarily
overthrown, meaning the right brain sneaks through
either in dream or when I let down my guard. Kant
knew zilch about the left brain and right, but he felt

that by theorizing the possible and testing it against
the actual, then wisdom might be increased. By now
the day is well advanced and I've spent the morning
in idle musing. A week of a cold snap and I'm eager
for a warm snap. Robins are back and I've seen rabbits
next door. Last year we had three adolescent rabbits
in our yard, but a redtail hawk got them all. Good
for the hawk, I expect, but it grieved me nonetheless.
Wonder can occur in the right brain and be blocked
by the left when a person is afraid of losing his sense
of consequence. So wonder might mean being struck
by sudden possibility or the presence of beauty, or that
parts of the known can combine to give a vivid sense
of the unknown. Even acts of kindness from unlikely
sources can cause it. But in the allocation of cerebral
labor the left brain worries and the right brain laughs;
so to shut down the right can make for heavy going.
My cynical friends thought wonder made them liable
to deception. How difficult to be open to possibility
when it threatens the self one has built from wisps
of smoke. Today on the river the ice appears thin,
the tide heaves it up and down; and brackish water takes
longer to freeze. Only an idiot would try to cross it.
Even so I'll drive over the bridge to the other side
and double back to the marsh where the rabbits might
have ended up. There I'll poke around like a man
looking for a lost coin on a sandy beach. I imagine
the chance of someone seeing me and asking: What

the heck are you doing? But I have my answer ready. I'm looking for a miracle, I'll tell him. Not that I think it will happen, I'm just keeping the possibility open.

NICKEL

This morning I awoke to find the furnace had shut down
in the night. Outside it was fifteen degrees and the wind
had blown every cloud from the sky. Inside even the dog
was shivering. The man at the oil company said happily:
You sure do use a lot of oil. To say that we keep the heat
turned low and the fireplace burning would have led him
to make ironic remarks, so I held my tongue and prepared
to pay another six hundred bucks. I think of the money
trickling back to the Mideast. A dollar here, a dollar there,
with the last few cents held in the hand of a man or woman
going to the market to buy bread—Iraqi, Saudi, or somebody
else. But isn't that how it works? Our money trickles down
all over the world and the last coin winds up in the hand
of somebody buying something small: bread, goat cheese,
shoelaces. Nearly every day the newspaper has a picture
of the results of a bomb blast in an Iraqi market, busted
cars and body parts tossed around. Today it's the Mideast,
though anyone with half a brain knows that pretty soon
the same scene will take place in Sydney or Dallas. We say
it'll never happen, but it's like telling a small lie, you get
a stretched feeling in your gut. Seattle, Hamburg, Paris—
you pick the spot, but in each place a few cents from my
two hundred gallons of oil will be tucked in somebody's

pocket or purse. I don't mean to be picky, if not this tank,
then the next. Or maybe today's coin will be Canadian,
Chilean, or German, who knows? I mean, have you ever
thought when holding a crumpled dollar bill how many
other hands have held it as well? It's too bad they can't
tag them like they tag geese, then on a computer screen
we could watch our dollar bills zigzag across the U.S.
Likewise my few cents making their way to a Baghdad
market, where after being turned into an Iraqi nickel,
it's blown a mile in the air — as for the hand that held it,
I don't want to think about it. Such ideas come to me
while I wait for the oil truck, but don't think I'm picking
on oil; it might be true of anything I buy, like anything
sizable. Often in the newspaper it's the juxtapositions
that upset me most — a photo of a blown-up market
next to an ad for Saks Fifth Avenue — a girl in skimpy
lingerie to make my mouth water, a street of body parts
to make it dry up. So is it better to see awful pictures
next to ads for funeral homes? It's hard to say. But today's
lack of heating oil is scarcely a tragedy. I'll sit by the fire
with the dog curled up nearby and mull over questions
like the ethics of living in a lucky spot when the world
is full of spots just the opposite. But shortly the oilman
will disrupt my thoughts, then I'll eat lunch and later
enjoy a therapeutic nap. Among the so-called primitive
people, tribes had intricate systems of taboo and mana,
bad luck versus good luck, with talismans and amulets
to guard them against the dark forces. How nice to have

a system of disconnected responsibility, to blame one
otherworldly power for being the cause of a problem
and to ask another otherworldly power to fix it. Wouldn't
we also be happier with clear-cut villains and defenders?
These days it's just a muddle as I think about my nickel
flying off to Baghdad or see a model in a minuscule bra
posed next to a severed head. I fret as much as I might
if I came down in the morning to find my furniture stuck
to the ceiling. No doubt I'd blink my eyes and say: Hey,
something's not right! How can I eat my poached eggs
with the refrigerator upside down and high above me?
So can I blame folks for watching four hours of junk
on TV each day? It's like hiding out in a secular church—
barbed wire between blessed ignorance and terror. Maybe
they don't pass the plate, but you have to watch the ads.
It seems whenever I start to ponder I fuss about bombs
and murder. And all this because my furnace stopped!
If not I might have written a poem about cats or taken
the dog for a walk. All I need is a jiffy between projects
A and B and I picture bombs in a Baghdad market. Can I
fix it, change it, or make it go away? No, I can only stare
in horror, as I might stand in a street watching a house
burn down, unable to act even if the house is my own,
until I get carpal tunnel just from throwing up my hands.
But when the oilman comes, I'll take the dog to the beach.
With a wind like the one last night, the waves in our part
of the ocean must be immense. I find it soothing to watch
the waves hammer one another, find it heartening to hear

their roar as spray is hurled high in the air and the waves
dash forward only to vanish and retreat as undertow,
before charging back to beat up the rocks. It creates
the illusion of life being fixed and problems sorted out.
Boom! Bang! But no harm done, really no harm done,
and when I've seen enough I'll go back to a warm house
telling myself I've completed significant work, even if
what I mean by work is just the good fortune to forget.

POSSUM

The English setter runs away across the cropped field
toward a break in the hedge. Eleven years old and she
has done this a thousand times. She means to browse
the local garbage cans as an aficionado of modern art
might browse a museum. I hurry after her, the clumsy
versus the nimble. Abruptly, she stops: a monster lurks
in her path. She backs up and shifts from side to side.
She doesn't even bark. It's a possum, her first possum,
hunkering motionless, but making a slight hissing noise.
I tug the dog away as the possum waddles to the brush.
Briefly, the dog has become a Christian. What did she
think she had found? A creature beyond her experience,
something going back a million years, as if I turned
the corner and came face-to-face with a Neanderthal—
not a time for friendly gestures. I've also seen foxes
in this field, but the possum survives with little more
than needlelike teeth and a knack for playing dead.
Like the porcupine and alligator it was well built
at the start and didn't need to evolve further, unlike
the dinosaurs that found safety by becoming birds.
What were our skills beyond an opposable thumb,
the ability to outlast any animal in the hunt, and a sense
of cause and effect? Once, when I was twenty, I took

a summer job with an oil company, going door-to-door
and handing out "free gifts": coupons for oil changes,
pencils, lollipops. Ten of us wore shirts advertising
the company's name and were roughly the same age.
One man, on his way to law school, used to brag about
his last job as a cashier in a market where he bought
food stamps from the poor at half price so they could
buy alcohol with the cash. He'd mock what he called
their stupidity and, despite my protests, he could find
no fault with what he'd done. He was short and squat
with a square head as if a huge hand had squashed him
down against the ground by about a foot. I wondered,
as I separated his action from the morality of his action,
if his trick was a survival tool like the skunk's stench,
a blankness of conscience that let him take advantage
of the poor and weak to save money for law school.
And how would he someday see that law, I thought,
would it be any more than an obstacle that he'd seek
ways to circumvent? The cropped field where I take
the dog is a small peninsula that pokes into the ocean
with a lighthouse at its tip. I call it Old Farts' Park,
since you must be at least sixty-five to drive your car
through the gate. Now it's part of Homeland Security
but staffed so rarely that terrorists could arrive daily
with nothing to hinder them but a hissing possum.
Venality, criminality, a readiness to go to any lengths —
is this what has let human beings survive, while those
who turned the other cheek were soon pushed aside?

Chekhov said, It's better to be a victim than a hangman,
a conception my co-worker of forty years back wouldn't
have grasped. Yet when I said he lacked a conscience,
he grew angry. He had a loving family, friends to whom
he was loyal, while those he robbed were hardly human.
This seemed another survival tool—he could rationalize
any action; like the president invading Iraq, it was right
because he thought it was right. His belief and desire
for it to be true became reason enough. But how many
would think it better to be victim rather than hangman?
In my truck with the dog sitting beside me on the seat,
I'm once more staring out at the winter ocean, drawing
solace or sustenance or a sort of calm from its seeming
permanence, though it, too, suffers a growing fragility.
A lyric poem can be a burst of emotion in one moment
of time and a narrative poem can employ its story line
to set up a lyric moment, but a meditative poem can be
a fretful thing, with dark musings coming and going
like crows weaving through winter trees. The students
to whom I speak of this tend to be timorous, more so
than thirty years ago, and men more than the women.
At times one writes a political poem that shouts a lot,
then he or she tears it up and returns to writing lyrics—
easier to write about fucking than to write about Iraq.
They feel ringed in by land mines of propriety, by issues
and attitudes, like my Honda Civic has been physically
challenged ever since I smashed it into a Mack truck.

Even if they burn to turn their passions into poems,
they feel they lack the right to speak freely. Chekhov
achieved his moral vision by what he called driving
the slave out of himself while still a teenager. Mostly
it meant ridding himself of thievery, pettiness, deceit,
and a readiness to flatter anyone with a little power.
It's hard for many students to do this—in fact, it's hard
for me as well—so they write poems on tiptoe, not all
but most, making fucking, fretting about the past, and
fussing over family matters the safest subjects. So who
am I to find fault? But it creates an apathy to poetry.
Maybe that's why I've been writing poems on subjects
mostly found in prose. I feel guilty pursuing the usual
material when the world hovers at the brink of collapse.
Is it nuts to think that each day safety gets farther away?
With all this talk the dog has fallen asleep. The waves
keep doing what they've done forever, and I hope
they never stop. As I dig a dog biscuit from the box,
the dog sits up. She thinks it's a reward for being good
and the past, if recalled, is now excused. Is this morality
posing as appetite or appetite posing as morality? Surely,
her lack of selflessness is also a survival tool. Then I see
a government truck stop by the gate. A man in uniform
climbs out and eyes me warily. I give him a cheery wave
as he walks inside. If I could make myself think he was
my own particular possum meant to balance out the dog's
earlier confrontation, a threat to set against her threat,

it might take my attention from a sillier misconception.
After all, with all the malcontents eager to lay waste
to the lighthouse, I'd like to think he's keeping me safe —
my personal survival tool is the sophistry of self-deceipt.

BALANCE

The other day I looked for Jimmy Hoffa's grave
(I didn't find it) as our southbound train sped through
the New Jersey Meadowlands buried beneath two
or three inches of snow — acres and acres of dead
marsh grass the exact color of Willie, a friend's
yellow Lab — and I thought, why shouldn't Jimmy's
skeletal hand be poking up there, too? But it wasn't,
or at least I didn't see it in the time it took the train
to pass. Jimmy was last glimpsed in the parking lot
of Machus Red Fox, a restaurant in Bloomfield Hills,
where I once went for lunch in my early twenties,
about nine years before Jimmy left us, prematurely,
after an apparent meeting with two mobsters, which
was the closest Jimmy and I ever got to becoming
acquainted, and, who knows, I might have saved him.
Stranger things have happened, although I never
thought of it till now. Once as a reporter, I watched
a seven-foot-tall Teamster thug called Tiny toss a guy
six feet off a picket line as if he were no more than
a wad of wet paper, so perhaps Jimmy and I might
never have been close — he being the Teamster boss.
But Jimmy's planting in the Meadowlands typified
a tough guy's attempt to fix a problem, and effectively,

it seems. My wife and I were traveling to D.C. to see
a bunch of paintings, a city I hadn't visited for at least
ten years. The White House and Capitol were ringed in
by more armed guards than hairs on a hog. And Al Gore
was in town to warn Congress about global warming
and was praised or sneered at along strict party lines,
but when Florida's voting machines are under ten feet
of water, then perhaps the Republicans will think again—
pardon the oxymoron. Attila (not the Hun) once said:
That's not me shouting, it's the earth that roars. While
Clarence Darrow said the only thing in life that ever
matched his expectations was a baseball game, which
is how I feel about certain paintings. I mean, Cézanne
and Vermeer were good in the way Stalin and Hitler
were bad; in the extremity of accomplishment they
towered over their competition. Hard to know who
was better or worse. You might think my comparison
somewhat frivolous, but if it weren't for the former,
why would I want to live in a world with the latter?
I have some friends who talk about a higher power,
which leads me to imagine a big guy with a big club
standing on a chair, but seeing Vermeer's painting
A Lady Writing a Letter makes me think that if
a flawed human being can create an object so closely
approaching the perfect, then perhaps there's hope
for the race as a whole, which is a notion I mostly
doubt and which I went to Washington to reaffirm.
In the painting a young woman in a yellow coat sits

at a desk lightly holding a quill to a sheet of paper
as she stares not at the viewer but a bit to the right,
as if pondering what word to put next, what word
exactly articulates her thought, a moment caught
three hundred and forty years ago and in the next
moment the correct word will strike her and she will
end her letter, though for all I know it's a grocery list.
All of Vermeer's thirty-five known paintings display
the same degree of calm, in contrast perhaps to having
eleven kids and the financial worry that killed him
at forty-three, none of which affects what makes us look
at these paintings and feel somewhat comforted in life
or to be offered a palpable example of the beautiful,
a word that mostly defies my definition, or an event
to set against Jimmy in the Meadowlands, if that indeed
is where he wound up, or the White House surrounded
by goons with big guns. By a higher power my friends
mean a power bigger than they are, by which they don't
mean the president or another human being; and for me
what Vermeer, Cézanne, and a bunch of others managed
to achieve matches that definition. Cézanne's painting
The Gardener Vallier is the exact opposite of *A Lady
Writing a Letter*. Old fart against beautiful woman, dark
against light, wide strokes against fine strokes, gobs
of paint against a thin sheen, although Vallier also
looks off as if trying to express a particular thought.
Yet one is equal to the other, and of course the same
quality may be found in books, music, in all the arts.

My years in Bloomfield Hills were a total confusion
so it's just as well Jimmy and I never became friends.
From twelve to twenty-four I was at war with everything
inside my head and my head was at war with everything
outside my head. But then life began to calm down,
although never enough to suit me, but I can't claim
the calming down was due to Vermeer or Cézanne,
even if I'd like to and even if in time they became part
of all I value. Looking at the White House was like
looking at an armed camp. People by the fence took
photos of one another with the White House a hundred
yards behind. I felt that whatever lived in that place,
whatever chewed, shat, worried, and perhaps thought
was contrary to what I held dear. It made me recall
Madrid in nineteen seventy-one seeing the Guardia Civil
outside Franco's palace or visiting Santiago in nineteen
eighty-one watching Pinochet's caravan of black cars
speed by. Like Hoffa and the men who killed him, these
were guys who felt that to be tougher made them safer.
Was that a world I could love or want to be a part of?
In Vermeer's painting *A Woman Holding a Balance*,
a young woman looks down at a small set of scales
held in her hand. The two gold pans are each the size
of a gold coin and are filled with nothing but light.
Behind her hangs a picture of the Last Judgment
with naked figures being slaughtered and dragged away.
The woman is offering a choice, as she weighs not coins
but spiritual matters. In fact, the painting is first of all

about light and mass, and only after that is it an allegory
about choice and how we are all weighed in a balance,
although I didn't grasp the allegory at first, only later
when we were on the train going north, and had already
passed through the Meadowlands and New York,
and were gliding along the edge of Long Island Sound
with afternoon light sparkling on the water. The snow
that had melted farther south began to reappear, first
in patches under the trees, then covering the ground,
but now it was gray and crisscrossed with footprints,
both animals and people, even strewn with litter. How
difficult to live within a balance, not to choose what
seems safe or makes me rich, but to lift the spiritual
worth of my life — a virtue I hardly understand or am able
to define, but it includes looking at Vermeer, Cézanne,
and other men and women also, as well as other works,
of art that is, though what art might consist of I've spent
my life trying to learn. Leaving the train in Rhode Island
on the second day of spring, I found the cold had returned
once again. In Washington, the daffodils were in flower
with the tulips soon to follow. But here yellow crocuses
were just starting to emerge through scraps of old snow,
each for its short life pushing upward with its head bent,
like a man with his shoulders bent under a heavy weight.

WEREWOLF

Last night I dreamt a jumbo jet fucked a werewolf bitch,
changed for the event into half-human form. Forgive me
if I begin on a personal note. The woman, or wolf, was not
dragged screaming to her fate, nor was she eager; rather,
as she lay on a bed with her knees up and her furry arms
stretched back behind her head, she seemed mildly content.
In the strange complexity of dreams, I'd had sex with her
not long before, and when she turned over on her belly
and offered up her butt, I'd been surprised; but then
I realized this was the way that other mammals, always
excepting dolphins, whales, and the occasional ape, partake
of sex, and being a werewolf what else would she know?
The bed rested on a platform in a grassy field around
which stood about thirty men and women who displayed
all the gravity of a church congregation. The sky was blue,
the weather balmy. The jet plummeted down at forty-
five degrees, making a dreadful racket. Right at the last
I ducked behind a rock, fearing the worst. Then came
a burst of light, an explosion and blast of wind. I guessed
the others had been toasted to a crisp, but this was not
the case, although they were scorched around the edges
and crept toward safety with befuddled looks. As for
the victim, she resembled an overcooked minute steak

and this seemed the point, for several men and women
of the congregation began to hand out plates and forks
as we prepared to eat the remaining scraps, hardly more
than bits of blackened meat. I didn't think we'd have
enough for all, but, as in the story of loaves and fishes,
we all ate our fill, though it tasted much as you'd expect.
A lady I'd never met said to me: What a terrible event!
I answered with a remark so apt it woke me from sleep:
Yes, but you'll never forget it. This account abbreviates
a narrative with all a dream's typical twists and turns,
none of which seemed strange at the time. And for me
it joined a lifetime of strange dreams, although this one
hit a highpoint. Even so I've seen a shrink, read Freud,
and the dream's sexual content seemed clear, that's to say,
I've reached the age when the beef torpedo is sometimes
transformed into pasta surprise — hence the jumbo jet.
And before going to sleep I'd been reading a book about
Saint Augustine at twenty studying literature at the university
in Carthage and joining the Manichaeans, whose rituals
were said to be odd. In my life, I've lived in fifteen states,
in at least forty apartments and houses, visited more than
twenty countries and lived in five or six. To these I add
the events experienced in books: Mr. Pickwick chasing
his hat, Anna Karenina's St. Petersburg — many hundreds
of books. And then I include dreams, not just fragments,
but dreams I can mostly recall with people I grow to love
who vanish in the morning; the many-roomed mansions
perched above the ocean, the faceless creature ascending

the cellar stairs. Each one has become part of who I am,
and of course teachers, lovers, friends, and even strangers
have added stories and the examples of their lives to this
repository of memory, a warehouse stuffed with packages
piled up to the rafters where no light will ever reach. So
a jumbo jet fucking a werewolf bitch is also part of me,
is part of the window through which I view the world.
How totally disgusting! a friend said. And I shrugged.
Why should I feel blame for what I dream? Yet looking
in the mirror I often ask: Who's in charge here? Because
at times it seems my body and conscious mind are a vehicle
run by a sensibility hidden far inside, like a man staring
at a computer in a post–nuclear war bunker. Don't say
this is Freudian metaphor; it feels like an absolute fact;
and in my mirror, I'm sure I see him back there tapping
his keyboard and tossing me an ironic look. The actor
Alastair Sim had two dream friends, a man and woman,
of whom he dreamt each night, and who became so close
he said the best part of his life took place while he slept.
Do others have similar dreams with imaginary friends
who appear night after night? Or some mornings I'll awake
out of sorts and I'll realize the reason is because a person
met in sleep has died, some accident or deep misfortune;
or I'll wake with delight as if in sleep I'd gotten a great gift.
Lately I dreamt I drove down tree-lined streets at dusk
trying to get around a ravine like the ravines in San Diego.
Soon came blocks of brick apartments, tall and nondescript.
Then, over a hill, I saw the end of the street ten yards ahead

with a wooden guardrail above the ravine. I hit the brakes,
but it was too late. The car split the barrier and twisted up
through the evening air. Below were rocks and cactus,
discarded trash, even an old refrigerator. I had no doubt
I'd be killed and I woke myself up stunned and panting.
For days those images have stayed with me, the shock
of the guardrail being so close, a sense of falling. So this
is how it will take place, I thought. But even if the dream
was purely metaphor, one part of the brain disclosing
a concern to the other, does that make the crash any less
of an event? The fear was my fear. It's not like a book.
When I was younger, my relation to my brain seemed
a pleasing mystery; now it's just a bother. My hopes,
plans — who's driving the car? People who think they're
in charge of their lives — is this more than vanity or pride?
This morning after dreaming of the werewolf and jet,
I drove to the lighthouse to study the water as I've done
many times this winter. Always the ocean has a different
character, like a person with a wealth of conversation
and behavior. Today the water seemed flat and leaden
and I saw no birds. Far off at the horizon two layers
of gray overlapped, and I stared out trying to determine
where the clouds stopped and sea began. These events
from which a life is built: I think how at the beginning
there was nothing, not quite a blank slate but almost,
a self waiting to become a self, a door open just a crack.
In "Voyage," the last poem in *Fleurs du mal,* Baudelaire
wrote, "For the child in love with maps and engravings,

the universe is the size of his vast hunger." Soon the child
starts out on life's journey as if on a ship, "pursuing
the infinite on the finite space of the seas." The weight
of memory and event in life's museum, in time its sheer
bulk defeats him. Then he prepares to sail again: "Death,
old captain," Baudelaire wrote, "we must hoist anchor.
If the sky and sea are as black as ink, our hearts are filled
with light." Today, thinking of my dream, trying to reach
some truce with myself and seeing the quiet of the water,
I thought the great expanse beneath the surface was like
the place my mind can't reach, while within the gray line
dividing ocean and sky lay the old doubts, the vagueness
and confusion, as if in their own country, and I wondered
if, like me, you have ever felt you lived out there: dusky
pathways, uncertain turnings, the dreamer and the dream.

LOOKING FOR THE DOG

This morning I saw my leg looked like the Leaning
Tower of Pisa, not the whole leg, just from the knee
to the foot, the right leg and bending away to the right.
Since then, I've thought of painting it a marble color
and sketching in those hundred or so little columns.
Wouldn't this be better than simply having a bad leg?
I'd be attaching myself to a tradition. And last week
after that singer cut her golden locks and some fellow
tried to sell them for a million dollars on the Internet,
I, too, had a haircut and I thought why not gather up
my gray locks and try to make two or three bucks?
Then I thought, what else have I got? Hammertoes,
three gold teeth, warts, and two stents in my heart,
couldn't they also go to the auction block? It might
at least be a way of linking with my fellow creatures,
becoming part of the great human family, from which,
so far, I've felt oddly distant. This is how my thinking
can swing toward self-deception; it gets all wound up,
with groundless ambition. But I need a distraction,
because two days ago the dog ran off, yet this time
she hasn't come back. And it's cold, the temperature
was down to zero. We phoned the police, the pound;
we drove up and down the streets. Even so, I saw it

as a rejection. She was bored without the kids around,
even depressed. She hated being at home by herself.
If I could have taught her to play cards, even Old Maid,
our relationship might have gotten better. This sense
of inadequacy that strikes me for ridiculous reasons,
where does it come from? It's as if it were out there
always waiting, like the flies outside the screen door,
one puncture in the mesh and they're rushing inside.
Moments later they're gobbling my lunch. It makes me
feel sorry for the president. I mean, if I at times find
myself at fault, he must be a wreck, given how badly
he's messed up. But have you ever met those people
who are so solipsistic they brag about their mistakes?
Right and wrong become just two different forms
of accomplishment. Maybe the president is like that
with all the dead soldiers he has to carry on his back.
Anyway, I've scoured the town looking for the dog.
Although winter, we've had little snow. This dog loved
garbage like Russians love caviar, and not only did she
sleep on the beds, but she crawled between the sheets.
And if I bought a box of chocolates, I'd have to hide it
on the top shelf of the closet otherwise she'd find it.
She chewed up ten of my wife's shoes, but just the shoes
for the left foot. My wife says that if I buy another dog,
she's moving out. The problem with having a knee
that looks like the Leaning Tower of Pisa is one day
it will have to go under the knife — that's what people
call a "known fact" — unless I croak first. Then I think

of other future troubles I've managed to block out,
like I never thought I'd have two stents in my heart.
In the operating room, the nurse asked, How d'you feel?
I said, I'd rather be in Pittsburgh. And she said, Oh,
do you have family in Pittsburgh? By then it was too late
to tell her about the scene where W.C. Fields is about
to be hanged and his witty response. At times I consider
the black door in my future and hear the wind whistling
under the crack. I used to think of it with dread, but now
I'm mostly curious, although I would hate to wind up
in a flaming car wreck, and also I've not yet been struck
by the terminal claustrophobia attending the increasing
constriction of life. But if the president sent those men
and women to Iraq for reasons of personal vanity, I hope
he never learns the truth, since how could he ever live
with himself? People I know who become suddenly rich,
even by accident, right away they feel important; they put
a swagger in their walk, see a superior face in the mirror.
That singer cutting off her golden locks thought she was
doing something as big as building the Brooklyn Bridge.
She thought the earth would screech to a halt. At times
it seems we're all a step away from being nuts, some being
closer than others. Would we have turned out smarter
if our primary competitor hadn't been the chimpanzee?
Just the other day my wife and a friend were saying
that when they were younger they felt sure in forty years
the world would have gotten better. But now that time
has gone past and they find the world is even worse.

How did it happen, they asked, was it arrogance, greed,
or self-deception? Really, I think the dog might be dead,
unless she was stolen, which I doubt. She could open
doors and sneak through small spaces so maybe this
was bound to happen, but we could have built fences
and given her more walks. Yet thinking it would never
take place was also self-deception, like saying my leg
is like the Leaning Tower of Pisa; I do it not to think
of my future beneath the knife. Does it ever strike you
that your mind is like someone else? I don't mean you're
psychotic, but your mind has one agenda and what you
call you has another? And even if you're completely
straightforward, your mind is devious and secretive?
So to say I'm running the show, that I'm the master
of my fate, is as far-fetched as flapping my ears really
hard to see if I can rise up a few inches from my chair.
Maybe this is about truth and how it seems accessible,
but what is accessible is the illusion of accessibility.
Driving through the dark and searching for the dog
is the way I go through life, although I try to think
it's summer and broad daylight. It's just like thinking
a thing is true because we wish it to be true, thinking
we're heading toward a future of green fields and babbling
brooks only to discover that we're heading for a cliff.
But thoughts like these, if I don't bring them to a halt,
make my doubts pile up, and the world looks so brief,
so fragile that I start poking my finger through its walls,
its seeming substantiality, as if through a wet tissue;

and if I don't repair my fabric of opinion and belief,
my illusion of truth, I'll drop like a rock from a roof,
falling, falling till I come to an abrupt stop. Like this.

CHAINSAWS

Chainsaws at dawn beneath a slate gray winter sky
as my neighbor's work crew clear-cuts the small lot
behind his house and next to mine, rhododendrons
and forsythia, junipers and spruce, and the mass
of prickly sweetbriar the cardinals like — despite
the rising ground and collection of rocks, he wants
an expanse of lawn as smooth as a putting green.
Maybe he lives here for one month in the summer.
When I phone him in Florida to protest, his wife
tells me: We've got twins, just toddlers, and I'm
afraid, you know, of bugs. Welcome to the world,
I want to say. Then, standing by an upstairs window,
I watch the sky let down its snow, just as leisurely
as these days I descend the stairs with my bad knee,
and one by one the chainsaws fall still. Two maples
and a rhododendron remain along the farther fence
so that, briefly, the lot grows virginal again, virginal
but shorn. With the chainsaws gone, the cat tiptoes
across his former hunting ground, an ascending line
of indentations leaving the cat's cryptic testimonial.
Will cardinals be safer if forced to build their nests
in higher places? Or does danger make them safer
by giving them a better measure of instructive risk,

just as a few bugs might fortify the twins next door?
Yesterday a woman told me she retained her calm
by never reading the papers or watching the news
on TV. For me the opposite is true, since if I don't
keep alert I'll think the world's bad luck will take
that moment to creep closer. Lately I read it wasn't
till the eighteenth century that Europeans thought life
was looking up and society's steady advancement
became a certainty in people's lives. Before then
the golden age lay far behind, and waiting ahead
lurked plague, devastation, and the Last Judgment.
A century later Whitman warbled about the future,
from the deck of the Brooklyn ferry, that in only
one hundred years other people would take delight
in the same sunset that he enjoyed. "As you feel
when you look upon the river and sky, so I felt."
But is this still the case? Don't we once again think
we face disaster? Barring the ignorant and apathetic
only the millenarians feel chipper as they get ready
to enter the promised land — a foolishness filling me
with eschatological anxiety. But three hundred years
from gloom to gloom seems severe. Three centuries
of feeling fortunate before the portal of opportunity
is slammed shut. But then, trying to dispel my fears,
I call the dog and we go to inspect the lot next door.
Eager for edible bounty, she zigzags across the yard
and sniffs the breeze as critics read *Ulysses,* seeking
a tasty subtext beneath the page itself. Nevertheless

I see the snow won't last. It's only several degrees
above freezing and by nightfall most will have melted.
It's just a taste of how winter used to be, three inches
of white speckled with soot from factories farther west.
But again I burden my observation with qualifications,
making each occasion a cause for political complaint.
Another writer claimed that prior to Christianity sin
didn't exist; it began with Zoroastrians and then was
taken up by Christians; meaning the Greeks, Romans,
and all the rest had only a sense of error. People suffered
serious flaws and oddball appetites. They had attacks
of bad luck, but Pandora freeing misery from its box
was just a mistake; Oedipus marrying his mom might
have happened to anyone. Doesn't this beat a president
calling a bunch of Arab terrorists "evil folks," people
whose numbers get bigger as the war in Iraq gets longer?
Well, unlike Whitman, no one will claim I've got a happy
warble as once again I resume my list of reservations.
The woman who swore off newspapers is always smiling,
but not like a kid with Down syndrome who's always
smiling. She's not challenged, as they say, rather she's
blessed with the bliss of the oblivious. You can't worry
about scary effects from scary causes if you don't care
to discover the nature of the causes. As the dog ascends
the drive next door, she grabs up mouthfuls of snow
and stops once or twice to pee. This is her chosen text
and she speed-reads the natural world according to what
she holds of value — food, danger, and sometimes sex.

But isn't the world my text as well, as if it didn't exist
until I'd turned it into language, although each word
I write lessens the precision of the thought? The map,
as Mr. Korzybski liked to repeat, is not the territory.
Or, as a friend said, I write because I've not yet heard
what I'm listening for. Then she said, quoting Heraclitus:
The mind hides from itself — by which she meant self-
deceit, and how can I see the truth if it's crisscrossed
by my own muddy footprints, or if the words I write
toss back my own reflection from the glass? As I look
at the lot where brush was cut, the cat's prints rising
to the top resemble a sentence detailing the day's events —
a tale with much left out. With a sudden leap, the dog
sprints through the gate, and just as I try to explicate
the world's enigmas, so she zigzags across the cat's
elegant design, editing the cat's remarks without adding
an iota of sense. Or do the cat's prints mimic my own
attempt to arrange my thoughts, while the dog's scrawl
is like the administration's mischief ringing in my ears,
their legalized illegality despoiling all my deliberation?
The most harmful American president since Jefferson
Davis, a friend said lately. But if I accept the sophistry
that danger makes me safer, then I should be happy
that the president turning Iraq into a terrorist camp
keeps me hopping as Dexedrine once kept me hopping.
And what would I like better? To listen to the whisper
of the natural world for the secret I hope to uncover:
the one the dog sniffs out when she studies the air;

the one the world's bluster and fear seek to obscure;
the one that to hear I must hush each voice within me;
the one I think must soon reveal itself, the one I think
will never reveal itself; the one I try to catch on paper—
hard to do that as I wait for a nuclear shoe to drop.
Why bother? one might inquire. Let me say how it was:
when I was young I was taken by a passion, and after
all this time I cling to it more firmly than ever. Luckily,
my task is only to pose the question, although today
it seems I patch together the absurd and far-fetched
seeking a scrap of comfort that I'm the first to doubt.
It's hard work to celebrate the world's bright variety
when full of hatred for the jackal's cynical chatter,
its easy demolition of the beautiful. Do I hide from
my thoughts or does my mind hide from my questions?
Right now the only certainty is my own uncertainty.
As the snow turns to rain, I hear a cardinal in the last
of the sweetbriar announce with its three-note attack
that it will be spring soon. Some things I must believe
even if each particle of flesh cries no. What peril, what
ravages lie ahead? I call the dog; we descend the hill.

SPRING

Out at the lighthouse a man with a yellow slicker
and a boy in a red jacket walk along the rocks
as I watch from my truck. The boy is about six —
father and son with their backs to me, hand in hand
and walking slowly, not talking — a scene repeated
maybe a trillion times since time began. My son
and I did that, too. When they negotiate the corner
to the front of the lighthouse, the boy looks back
to his mother waiting in the parking lot and makes
a small wave just to let her know he's okay. Today
is April 1st. At one point I started to shout: Hey, kid,
your pants are on fire! But then I thought I'd better
not, the parents might get upset, maybe report me.
You can never tell these days. Everyone is looking
at everyone else, wondering what they'll do next,
like pull a knife, and if that doesn't worry them,
maybe it should. The water is gunmetal blue and
as flat as a blanket; some fog on the horizon keeps
the foghorn busy. And today is a friend's birthday,
maybe a former friend. I last saw her and her husband
in Rome, meeting in front of the Pantheon. The day
was hot; the square, crowded. We had coffee and
discussed old friends: who was well, who was not.

My wife and I had just spent a month in Florence,
a daily round of paintings and cappuccinos. Now
we're bickering about money. That's how it goes,
a pendulum giving what's called character to a face,
or carving a road map to a place not worth the trip.
From my truck I can see the tip of Long Island.
I've a friend over there I haven't seen for a while,
maybe a former friend. I'm afraid I've got too many
of those. The ones who remain, the ones who are gone,
those in between—I miss them all. Once my feelings
fix on a person, they stay bright pictures in my mind,
they always stay fresh even if I never see them again.
Often that feels like a weight. In Florence I saw that
Savonarola and Anna Akhmatova had the same nose,
long with a distinctive bend a third of the way down.
Akhmatova felt that Florence represented everything
opposite to Russia under Stalin and this protected her
and her poetry. She began to write at the age of eleven
and Savonarola, too, wrote poetry when young, but then
told his father he couldn't stand "the blind wickedness
of the people of Italy," which led him into the church
and to Florence as a puritan preacher where he created
a democracy, a gift too costly for the city's wealthy
and the pleasure-seeking church. When the pope tried
to bribe him with a cardinal's hat, Savonarola replied:
"A red hat? I want a hat of blood." And so he was hanged
with two others and the bodies burned in the Piazza
della Signoria. My wife's niece visited us in Florence,

a woman so lovely that men stumbled over their feet
as she passed. She liked having her photo taken in front
of public statues, other places also, often asking people
to take her picture with her camera, which made me see
the spot that moved me most was the plaque showing
where Savonarola had been burned, because she didn't
want her picture taken there—it being only a metal
circle set into the stones. Staring down at the plaque,
I was sure I felt the preacher and former poet burn.
This morning two men in a boat set out lobster pots.
The Block Island ferry from New London cruises past
on a straight line, a no-nonsense sort of work. I can see
few birds: one resembling a miniature goose, practicing
dives, and some gulls hunting for snacks. A movie I saw
last night about East Germans spying on one another
in the early eighties was about complicity, how everyone
was guilty in a system that ensnared them and everyone
they loved as hostages. Hard not to squeal like a stuck pig
and sell out your neighbors and lovers and best friends
with your own life on the line. Even Anna Akhmatova
at last caved in. Her poetry condemned; accused of being
half harlot, half nun; her first husband shot as a traitor,
another husband rotting in prison. Then, with her son
in Siberia, she sought to get him back by writing poems
in praise of Stalin: "Where Stalin is, we have Freedom,
Peace, and grandeur on earth." Was her betrayal of what
led her to write a knife in her gut all the rest of her life?
Or did she say: I was forced to do it because of my son.

That's the trouble with complicity, the lesser of two evils
may be only a bit better than the greater. Even Savonarola
bargained with the pope and shut his mouth to protect
his work, which did little good since he still got hanged.
But both were lucky to have identifiable villains. Here
we're bought by having sugar poured down our throats,
in a country distrusted by every other country on Earth,
and a widening program of spying on our own people.
This just begins the list as we say complicity doesn't exist.
Yet all my actions reek of complicitous acceptance. Is it
wrong to live in comfort when so many die in Darfur? I
expect it is. Today I've little room in my heart for anything
but complaint; it becomes my illness and great discontent.
The smoke from Savonarola's corpse must have coated
the windows of that lovely square with a greasy film.
When I looked from the Palazzo Vecchio, I was sure
the distortions in the glass were caused by the smoke
from the victims burned below. I'd think of it at night
till I thought I was going nuts. Freud said the neurosis
of thinking the wretchedness around us doesn't exist
lets us stay sane, although at times it seems that sanity
comes at too great a cost, so even the joy of walking
with one's son along the ocean's edge extracts its price
in drops of blood. A year before being hanged, Savonarola
held a Bonfire of the Vanities at the same spot: books,
silk dresses, musical instruments all went up in smoke.
Botticelli even tossed in two of his own paintings.
This excess rivals the excess of Savonarola being hanged,

one more pendulum swing to give character to a face.
Isn't a withdrawal from friends a withdrawal from life
and a denial of time's assaults? Better to preserve them
as bright pictures in my mind than to see them vanish
into the dark. Akhmatova's love of Florence included
Dante and his poetry, and this, too, she set against Stalin,
not that it justified her complicity, but it offered relief.
Don't say it was only a distraction, only another vanity.
Perhaps it formed the gift that let her gain back Freud's
cleansing neurosis, to live in the presence of the horror
even if it meant pretending that the horror didn't exist.
If answers are excuses, is art a more acceptable excuse
or is it just a twig I put down to tiptoe across the muck?
Now the boy in the red coat has worked his way around
the lighthouse and comes running back to his mother,
imagining her concern, as his father comes trailing after.
For a while she is the boy's whole world till he graduates
to the larger world that year by year will carve his story
across his face. What compromises will he have to make
with how he wants to live? But today my hopes are set
on the start of spring as the gods of a hundred religions
are being reborn, yearly visitors who give the world
a penetrating look, receive our praise, and briefly offer
their consoling warmth, before they once again depart.

LOST

A cry was heard among the trees,
not a man's, something deeper.
The forest extended up one side
the mountain and down the other.

None wanted to ask what had made
the cry. A bird, one wanted to say,
although he knew it wasn't a bird.
The sun climbed to the mountaintop,

and slid back down the other side.
The black treetops against the sky
were like teeth on a saw. They waited
for it to come a second time. It's lost,

one said. Each thought of being lost
and all the years that stretched behind.
Where had wrong turns been made?
Soon the cry came again. Closer now.

ABOUT THE AUTHOR

Stephen Dobyns has published thirteen books of poems, twenty novels, a book of essays on poetry (*Best Words, Best Order*) and a book of short stories (*Eating Naked*). Ten of his novels form a series of mysteries set in Saratoga Springs, New York. His first book of poems, *Concurring Beasts,* was the Lamont Poetry Selection of the Academy of American Poets. *Black Dog, Red Dog* was a winner in the National Poetry Series. *Cemetery Nights* received the Poetry Society of America's Melville Cane Award.

He has received fellowships from the Guggenheim Foundation and the National Endowment of the Arts, as well as numerous awards for individual poems. Two of his novels, *Cold Dog Soup* and *The Two Deaths of Señora Puccini,* have been made into films. Dobyns was a general assignment reporter for the *Detroit News,* and he has been a contributing writer for the *San Diego Reader* since 1995. He has taught at many colleges and universities, including the University of New Hampshire, Boston University, the University of Iowa, Brandeis Univesity, Syracuse University, and Sarah Lawrence College.

Stephen Dobyns lives with his wife in Westerly, Rhode Island, and teaches in the M.F.A. Program at Warren Wilson College.

Lannan Literary Selections

For two decades Lannan Foundation has supported the
publication and distribution of exceptional literary works.
Copper Canyon Press gratefully acknowledges their support.

LANNAN LITERARY SELECTIONS 2010

Stephen Dobyns, *Winter's Journey*

Travis Nichols, *See Me Improving*

James Richardson, *By the Numbers*

John Taggart, *Is Music: Selected Poems*

Jean Valentine, *Break the Glass*

RECENT LANNAN LITERARY SELECTIONS
FROM COPPER CANYON PRESS

Michael Dickman, *The End of the West*

James Galvin, *As Is*

David Huerta, *Before Saying Any of the Great Words: Selected Poems,*
translated by Mark Schafer

Sarah Lindsay, *Twigs and Knucklebones*

Heather McHugh, *Upgraded to Serious*

W.S. Merwin, *Migration: New & Selected Poems*

Valzhyna Mort, *Factory of Tears,* translated by Franz Wright
and Elizabeth Oehlkers Wright

Taha Muhammad Ali, *So What: New & Selected Poems, 1971–2005,*
translated by Peter Cole, Yahya Hijazi, and Gabriel Levin

Lucia Perillo, *Inseminating the Elephant*

Ruth Stone, *In the Next Galaxy*

Connie Wanek, *On Speaking Terms*

C.D. Wright, *One Big Self: An Investigation*

For a complete list of Lannan Literary Selections from
Copper Canyon Press, please visit Partners on our Web site:
www.coppercanyonpress.org

The Chinese character for poetry is made up of two parts: "word" and "temple." It also serves as pressmark for Copper Canyon Press.

Since 1972, Copper Canyon Press has fostered the work of emerging, established, and world-renowned poets for an expanding audience. The Press thrives with the generous patronage of readers, writers, booksellers, librarians, teachers, students, and funders—everyone who shares the belief that poetry is vital to language and living.

Major funding has been provided by:

Amazon.com

Anonymous

Beroz Ferrell & The Point, LLC

Golden Lasso, LLC

Lannan Foundation

National Endowment for the Arts

Cynthia Lovelace Sears and Frank Buxton

William and Ruth True

Washington State Arts Commission

Charles and Barbara Wright

For information and catalogs:

COPPER CANYON PRESS
Post Office Box 271
Port Townsend, Washington 98368
360-385-4925
www.coppercanyonpress.org

Winter's Journey is set in Baskerville 10, a digital reworking of the eighteenth-century English type of John Baskerville by František Štorm. Book design and composition by Valerie Brewster, Scribe Typography. Printed on archival-quality paper at McNaughton & Gunn, Inc.